CATHEDRAL
CATS

Richard Surman

Fount
An Imprint of HarperCollins*Publishers*

To the memory of Steve Abis,
a man of principles and great courage, who loved cats.

Fount Paperbacks is an Imprint of
HarperCollins*Religious*
Part of HarperCollins*Publishers*
77–85 Fulham Palace Road, London W6 8JB

First published in Great Britain
in 1993 by HarperCollins*Religious*
This edition first published in 1997 by
Fount Paperbacks

1 3 5 7 9 10 8 6 4 2

Richard Surman asserts the moral right to be
identified as the author and photographer of this work

A catalogue record for this book is
available from the British Library

0 00 628071 4

Printed and bound in Hong Kong by
Paramount Printing Co. Ltd

CATHEDRAL
CATS

Contents

Introduction

When I was invited to work on a book called *Cathedral Cats*, I leapt at the idea. For one thing I am a cat lover. When I was a child, my father, an otherwise quiet and dignified man, would walk around the house with a long length of string trailing from his waistband to provide entertainment for them. William, one of our earlier cats, ate my newts. Bodger, the grandest and most regal tabby of the house, was a glutton. We found him one night, ankle deep in the middle of a large dish of rice pudding, eating it as fast as he could.

I also have a passion for architecture, sacred and secular, which has found me, in my work for the Westminster Abbey Preservation Trust, teetering along the apex of the Abbey nave, and hanging from the West towers.

Further, I knew there would be plenty of subjects. Most cathedrals have cats. When I began to pursue them, however, I was amazed at how the tamest and most sociable animals are nevertheless completely independent and sublimely unpredictable. The contrast between the landscapes I am accustomed to photographing, which generally stay very still, and these errant cats couldn't have been more marked.

We polled most of Britain's cathedrals to find out if they had cats. The cathedrals which don't appear generally didn't have. Our initial research revealed that one cat which we had banked upon using – Thomas à Becket at Llandaff – was too infirm to take part. Toast, at Lincoln Cathedral, had been banished in disgrace for spraying the nave pillars. The splendid, if cantankerous, Biggles had met a similar fate after he scratched one tourist too many. Rusty and Ug were just about to retire with their owners the Hipples at Bristol.

If these had been the only obstacles, it would have been an easy piece of work. In the event, I decided to photograph the cats in as natural a way as possible and, frankly, paid for it. At St Albans it poured with rain for much of the day. When we eventually got Ambrose out, he spent about three hours under some parked cars and then he climbed up a large yew tree. As I sat patiently awaiting his descent he slipped quietly over a wall. I resolved to add a pair of binoculars to my kit.

The saga of disappearing cats continued at Ely. Skimbleshanks vanished as soon as I appeared. I tracked Marmaduke scuttling down the High Street to a piece of waste ground, where he streaked up an old bay tree. He stretched out on a branch for the next three hours. Sir Galahad, at Canterbury, took one horrified look at me and disappeared behind a radiator.

It was a wildlife photo-safari at Coventry, where I listened for the sounds of Truffles and his relatives in the undergrowth and tried to stay concealed. In

Peterborough I wouldn't have got any photographs of Sammy had it not been for Keith Nelson, armed with a large bag of turkey scraps.

But there were roses amongst the thorns. Dennis at St Paul's almost seemed to ask me how to stand, and after two days of photography we were becoming good friends. Biggles too, despite his fearsome reputation, was pretty tolerant, although he totally ignored the smoked salmon I had stuck on the back of some ivy leaves to delay his departure through a window.

Taking all of February and most of March, with my car clocking up around seven thousand miles, the trip around the cathedrals was epic. On location I must have presented a strange sight to tourists. At Westminster, I lay full stretched on the pavement in Dean's Yard. At Gloucester I crouched by Gorbachev's miniature archway like a cat paparazzi.

I thought I'd be meeting some magnificent purebred cats. In fact the only pedigree was Chandos, the Siamese at St Davids. Almost all the others had been rescued somehow. They were, if you like, charity cats. I thought it rather fitting that places which exist for the glory of God have become homes to the orphaned, neglected and mistreated of some of his lesser creatures – the cathedral cats.

Planning and researching the book was not easy, and without the invaluable encouragement and support of my editor, Giles Semper, and his assistant, Lindsay Armstrong, it would have been almost impossible. Both Giles and I received great encouragement and support from the late Steve Abis, then Art Editor at HarperCollins and an inspirational person.

Sheba & Min of Winchester

Carlisle

York

Lincoln

Peterborough
Ely

Worcester   Coventry
Hereford
Gloucester   St Albans
              Christ Church
St Davids   St Paul's
                              Westminster
                    Bristol   Canterbury
Wells
        Salisbury   Winchester

Exeter

Truro

MAP SHOWING THE SITES
OF THE CATHEDRALS

Rusty & Ug

When a large colony of mice were disturbed
by building work at Bristol cathedral school nineteen
years ago, the pest controller had only one piece
of advice. 'Get a cat' he said.

The Head Verger Rex Hipple and his wife Elsie were told of a litter of tortoiseshell kittens at a farm in the Mendips. Rusty was selected and conveyed to her new home with the Hipples, a diminutive bundle of fluff, half the size of the milk bottles next to which she liked to sit. The mice, at the first whiff of a cat, completely disappeared.

Bristol cathedral has an unusual mixture of Norman, Early English and Victorian architecture. Augustinian canons built the original Abbey church, which was granted cathedral status under Henry VIII. The twelfth century Chapter House has splendid arcades and vaulting and the central vault has a curious feeling of sideways space, accidentally engendered by the unique flying buttresses and cross arches. There is an interesting collection of abbots' effigies as well as medieval glass and Renaissance and Georgian monuments.

Rusty showed not the slightest embarrassment at being unable to fulfil her ordained function as mouse hunter. Instead she spent many happy hours exploring the eight-hundred-year-old barrel vault cloisters. Another favourite haunt was the workshop, which ran right under the old deanery. Most cats would run a mile from the din, with lathes, saws and other machinery going full blast, but not Rusty. She'd saunter in, often getting locked up for the night when the men had finished work.

Ug arrived in a far more dramatic fashion, as a feline waif and stray. One freezing night the Hipples were disturbed by a knock at their front door. A chorister was standing outside, holding a tiny brown, black and white kitten, which he thought belonged to them. It didn't and the chorister left, taking the kitten with him.

It was quite by chance that Elsie Hipple happened to glance out of her front window a few minutes later to see the kitten being set down and left in the frost covered grass by the West End of the cathedral. Convinced that it wouldn't survive, the Hipples' son David went out

Ug and the Victorian gatehouse

and brought it back. Never having seen such a tiny kitten, Elsie called it 'Little Cat'. Rex had noticed the length of its whiskers, however, and felt that it would grow to be anything but little. He promptly renamed it Ugly, or 'Ug' for short.

Rusty made Ug's life hell at first, chasing her up and down the stairs until Ug would simply give up, exhausted. Then came the inevitable day when Ug suddenly realized that she was in fact larger than Rusty, and the roles were abruptly reversed.

Photographing the aged Rusty was a rather touching experience. She is not very steady on her legs, and

The foundling Ug

Frail Rusty in the winter sun

when I picked her up and 'posed' her, she stood wobbling slightly and purring loudly, happy to oblige as far as she could. It seemed kinder to lay her down, where she was much more comfortable, and to take my pictures as unobtrusively as possible.

Adored equally by the Hipples' daughter Julia, Rusty and Ug differ strongly in one respect. Rusty detests being taken away, whereas Ug is a born traveller. Whilst Rusty remained to keep an eye on the cathedral, Ug would travel up to Scotland, visiting David at university, or staying in the family's favourite harbour wall cottage in the fishing port of Dunbar. Rex recalls how Ug would sit all day, watching the fishing boats, the lifting bridge and seagulls with intense interest.

Ug also went on a canal holiday, walking nonchalantly down the towpath to the barge, and hopping aboard with the ease of an ancient mariner. She wasn't quite so sure of herself one morning when she was woken by the sound of tapping on the side of the boat, and discovered that two large and hungry swans were to blame. She fled in alarm, deciding that discretion was the better part of valour.

Sir Lancelot & Sir Galahad

Only one of these two brother cats –
Sir Galahad – has the bold and fearless nature of
an Arthurian knight. It is he who has done battle with
Polly, a pretender to their territory from the
neighbouring choir house.

As the battles raged, Sir Lancelot merely mewed encouragement from behind the drawing room window. Although Sir Galahad was always victorious, the truce may only be temporary.

While there is peace, the two cats lord it over the East End of the precincts. They show no particular interest in visiting other residents, but seek out the company of the research archivist. Perhaps they want to know why they are the bearers of such distinguished names. Then again, old books and papers are good for the sharpening of claws.

Lancelot and Galahad are nine years old, but they are not the first cats to have shared the household of the Dean, John Simpson. When the family moved to Canterbury twelve years ago, they knew cats would be in clover in the medieval precincts. A visit to the RSPCA yielded not one but two ginger kittens, which they named Tiddles and Tiny Tiddles.

When Tiny Tiddles unexpectedly died of leukemia, the family went back to the RSPCA for another cat. Again they emerged with two kittens – black this time – which had been rescued from under a hedge near a farm. The children were reading the Arthurian legends at the time, and insisted that they be named after two of the most valiant knights.

Tiddles steadfastly refused to have anything to do with the two new arrivals, but then succumbed to the same illness as his brother, and was buried in the deanery garden.

When John Simpson was appointed Dean of Canterbury, the family had to move from one part of the cathedral precinct to another. Knowing that

Galahad the brave; Lancelot the timid

without some form of acclimatization the cats would keep returning to their old home, the family came up with a bright idea. Sir Lancelot and Sir Galahad were chivvied into cat baskets over two days, put in the car, and driven gently around the precincts. Pleased with their accomplishment, the family released the two cats – who promptly ran straight back to their old house.

Not surprisingly, it was food that persuaded them to move into their new quarters. Nowadays Sir Galahad greets the visitors with a bold display of friendliness, while Lancelot peers out from his favourite vantage point behind a radiator.

ABOVE: *Lancelot in his redoubt*
RIGHT: *Galahad stands guard against Polly*

Bessie, Rosie & Tabby

'Bessie is an aristocat', says her owner,
Canon Jenkins of Carlisle Cathedral, distinguishing
her from his two other cats, Rosie and Tabby.
Certainly she accepted with equanimity his
translocation from St Cuthbert's parish church
over the wall to the Cathedral.

Carlisle Cathedral is actually something of a wildlife sanctuary, with rabbits, a colony of dormice, hedgehogs and a wide variety of birds, including birds of prey. Founded in 1122, and battered by centuries of Border warfare, the cathedral was partly demolished to provide material for the fortification of the town walls. Despite its comparative smallness, it has a particular charm and beauty. There is a magnificent fourteenth century East window, and fascinating medieval paintings in the North and South aisles showing scenes from the life of St Augustine.

Bessie is most prominent at Christmas. Excited children can be heard telling their parents that, together with the donkey, and the cattle, there's a real cat curled up in the straw crib next to the infant Jesus. Little do they know that, for every afternoon she spends in the cathedral crib she spends another tucked up in the St Cuthbert's crib next door.

One Christmas Eve during a live television broadcast, Canon Jenkins was confronted by a distraught television producer. A cat was wandering in and out of shot, and he wanted it removed immediately. A few minutes later the same producer rushed up to him again. Contritely he explained that, as they were

Bessie: owl or pussycat?

having so many 'phone calls from viewers expressing their delight at Bessie's presence, could she please be readmitted. A string quartet who regularly broadcast from the cathedral have made it a *sine qua non* that Bessie is present during recordings.

She meets this tolerance with a high degree of sensitivity and tact. One night, the Julian group met for an evening of prayer. Bessie quietly opened the door to their meeting room, slipped in and lay quietly on the group leader's lap until they were finished. Canon Jenkins remembers with affection how she stayed constantly with his wife Rose when she developed a fatal illness.

Unfortunately Bessie's amiability was at a premium on the day she was photographed. Having been tracked to a wonderful position on a wall, she watched as the camera was lined up before springing down on the other side.

Bessie, like Ambrose at St Alban's, originally came from a farm – a Scottish one in her case. The farmer's wife insisted on inspecting the canonry to ensure its suitability before allowing Bessie to come. When she did, it was to join two other cats, Albert and Plato. Albert, for whom the bell for evensong was an irresistible summons, is believed to have passed on much of his love for cathedral life to Bessie. He would have nothing to do with her however, until she had been purged of all trace of farm odour.

When Canon Jenkins eventually remarried, his new wife Kathy brought with her two tabby cats, Rosie and

Bessie in full retreat

Tabby. She was shocked to find that Bessie was fed on choice chicken pieces. Rosie and Tabby are farm cats, and Kathy vowed they would never be pampered like Bessie. Unfortunately the rarified atmosphere of the cathedral has taken hold of the cats, and Tabby is now always first in line for the chicken.

There may be three cats in the deanery, but they all live in fear of Dandy, the pub cat, whose reputation for thuggery is unrivalled in the area. The noise created when he tries to bluster his way through the Jenkins' cat flap is perhaps the unholiest to be heard at Carlisle Cathedral.

LEFT: *Tabby, through a glass darkly*

Maisy

Maisy lives in the house where Alice Liddell, the Alice of *Alice in Wonderland* and *Alice through the Looking Glass*, spent her childhood. The author Charles Dodgson (Lewis Carroll) taught mathematics in the college.

*The room that held
the Looking-Glass*

When she arrived, she showed only a passing interest in the gardens, where the door which features in Alice's shrinking and growing episodes is to be found. Perhaps she sensed the spirit of the Cheshire Cat grinning down at her from the horse chestnut tree in the garden. Rather, she followed her master – John Drury, Dean of Christ Church – around constantly for security. Only recently has she made the oak panelled comfort of Alice's nursery her own.

In coming to Oxford Maisy trod the well-worn academic path between the universities of Cambridge and Oxford. She began life humbly, however, in the Blue Cross hospital in Cambridge. Her first experience of the outside world was in the Drurys' garden on the opposite side of the River Cam from King's College, where John Drury was also Dean.

From the time of her arrival, Maisy was 'one of the gang' with the children, tearing around the garden in a frenzy, leaping up and down trees, and taking the occasional break to go and find the headmaster of King's College school's cat, with whom she frequently skirmished.

When inside, which was not often in those days, Maisy would wait for one of Mrs Drury's theology students to come for a tutorial, wander into the study, and scramble up onto the student's lap, where she'd sit attentively. She kept up this particular habit when Mrs Drury resumed her tutorials at Oxford.

The cathedral to which she is now attached is unusual. It is England's smallest, and also serves as a college chapel to Christ Church. Originally a priory church built by Augustinian monks, it retains traces of the Norman structure. Most of the stonework dates from about 1170.

On one of her rare excursions out of the house, Maisy became pregnant. Mrs Drury recounts how,

close to giving birth to her kittens, Maisy saw the family in the process of going out of the front door. She leaped over and clung for dear life to Mrs Drury's leg, dragging her back in. So Maisy had her midwife, and the Drurys had a litter of kittens.

One reason for Maisy's reluctance to leave the house could be the squirrels in nearby Christ Church Meadow. Responding perhaps to a population explosion, they have colonized the deanery gardens, chewing the buds off the Cheshire Cat's tree and generally making a nuisance of themselves. They have also invaded the kitchen looking for food through the cat door; there was evidence of a vicious and bloody battle with Maisy. The arrival of Toby the dog put paid to the squirrel incursions, but posed a new problem for Maisy, who finds him over-friendly.

When I visited Maisy she showed no reluctance to go outside and, like the Cheshire Cat, to disappear. On my second visit she was much more cooperative to the extent of accompanying me for the first time ever through Alice's door into the cathedral grounds. The problem was then to get her back in. We were unwittingly assisted by the appearance of Toby the Dog, at which Maisy streaked back into the house.

When squirrels and dogs are distant threats and she is happy, Maisy can be easily located in the house. Of all the cats in this book, she has the loudest purr.

Wonderland: a first visit to the garden

LEFT: *Maisy ventures through Alice's door*

Truffles & Friends

Coventry Cathedral is an Anglican establishment,
but has a colony of feral cats that would be the boast
of any monument in Rome. Perhaps this multicoloured
tribe can trace its ancestry back to medieval times,
when the church of St Michael – the original
cathedral – was founded

The combination of gardens, overgrown corners and the ruined cathedral provide an extensive territory for feral cats. Sir Basil Spence's 1962 cathedral sits alongside the ruins of the original, which was destroyed by fire bombs in a protracted air raid during the Second World War. The new cathedral is bold, simple and coherent, and combines considerable architectural vision with works by a number of well known artists. John Piper's stained glass, Graham Sutherland's huge tapestry, and the engraved glass wall of John Hutton adorn the interior, whilst outside Jacob Epstein's statue of St Michael and the Devil has become a familiar symbol of the cathedral.

The cats' story is ably told by Mrs Mary Ford, manageress of the cathedral bookshop, who has cared for the cats for all the ten years she has worked there.

A sentinel looks out

Truffles braves sticks and stones

One day, glancing through her office window, Mary happened to notice a mother cat shepherding a litter of kittens along a path in the long disused gardens at the back of Cathedral House. She was particularly concerned to see that one of the kittens had a deformed hind leg.

She persuaded Canon Peter Berry to prise open a disused door into the garden, and pushed through the undergrowth to the spot where she had last seen the cat and kittens. It was deserted. Then Mary noticed a large gap beneath the ground floor of the building, behind a neglected flower bed. She peered inside. Staring back at

her was not one mother cat, but the startled eyes of more than fifty feral, stray and abandoned cats and kittens. Mary describes how eerie it was to see all those unblinking eyes watching her from the gloom.

She resolved to observe more closely and frequently, to get an idea of the extent and condition of this large feline colony. It quickly became clear to her that many of the cats were in a poor state, and in some cases half starved. Mary started a programme of feeding, and quickly became known as 'Mary the cat lady'.

Katie, one of the Cat Protection League committee members, came to hear of Mary's endeavours. She began to raise funds for cat food and proposed that a programme of neutering was needed, if the colony was to avoid an uncontainable population explosion. The League fieldworker, Mrs Pauline Simmons, supplied traps and baskets, and soon Mary was busy delivering irate cats to and from the CPL.

Mary also set about finding homes for many of the cats, and reduced the resident population to about twenty. Two were particularly distinctive. One was the cat with the deformed leg, who was known as Hoppy. After several futile efforts, he was trapped and the leg was successfully amputated. He convalesced in the then Provost's house, where he hissed at anyone who entered his room until the day he was released.

Another was the cat who allowed Mary near her to treat her eyes, and which she called Truffles. Not much is known about her, other than that, unlike the others, she doesn't confine herself to the old garden, taking a daily patrol through the bombed out remains

of the old cathedral, round the new building and back to her garden.

Mary has built small wooden shelters for the remaining cats, who now luxuriate nightly in their own accommodation, complete with old clothes in which to bed down. Truffles, however, has decided that old clothes don't quite provide the degree of comfort she would like, and has lined her shelter with the very best of pigeon's feathers.

Taking pictures of Truffles and her sidekicks was one of the hardest photographic tasks involved in this book. Only once, when she sat on the window of the room which I had made my initial observation post, was it easy.

It is however quite an experience to walk through the deserted gardens, catching the odd glimpse of a cat lurking in the undergrowth. It is quite an experience too to watch how the cats accept Mary as their benefactor and guardian.

LEFT: *A wild cat of Coventry*
RIGHT: *Truffles safe behind glass*

Marmaduke & Skimbleshanks

Marmaduke and Skimbleshanks have
had an education. Their young guardian Sara,
together with a neighbour's daughter, set up
a unique feline training school.

Marmaduke on the defensive...   *...and about to pounce.*

The object of the exercise was to make the two wanderers, second only to Dennis of St Paul's in this respect, a little more home loving. Each cat was given a doll's cot, to which they dutifully return to this day.

After much patience, the two teachers also had the two cats trundling around the cathedral precincts in a pram. For Marmaduke and Skimbleshanks it was no doubt an easy way to survey further opportunities for exploration.

Sara is the daughter of Paul Trepte, director of music at Ely, and his wife Sally. They live in a house overlooking the North transept and octagonal lantern tower of Ely Cathedral. This feature, unique to an English cathedral, replaced the Norman central tower, which collapsed in 1323. The site was originally a Benedictine Abbey, dating back to pre-Norman Conquest times, and many of the monastic buildings were severely damaged during the time of the Dissolution. Remnants of Abbot Simeon's great Abbey church are still to be seen in the cathedral, and there is a shrine to St Ethelreda.

Both two years old, ginger Marmaduke and tabby Skimbleshanks originally came from the local Cat Protection League. Well schooled they may have been, but they continued to wander where their whiskers led them, either individually or as a team. They became acquainted with the large rabbit that lives in the garden. They both befriended the Head Verger, and began to accompany him on his evening patrols, waiting patiently whilst he locked doors and gates.

Their particular interest lies in shopping, and both cats call by the cathedral shop in the high street.

Skimbleshanks seems to prefer clothes shops, into which he strolls, tail twitching in greeting. He favours one knitwear shop in particular, and the shop assistant regularly calls the Treptes to let them know where their tabby is. He did rather overextend himself one night, ending up on the far side of town, pleading to be let in to a complete stranger's house.

Marmaduke generally prefers shoe shops but, unbeknownst to Skimbleshanks, he also makes surreptitious visits to the local pet shop, where he cajoles cat treats out of the proprietor. When I tried to photograph him he led me through the traffic and the bustling shoppers with barely a sideways glance.

Expert at spotting open windows and doors in the cathedral precinct, the two cats often slip quietly into a neighbour's house for a peaceful and usually undetected night's sleep. Marmaduke in particular adjourns to a house which offers bed and breakfast, presumably hoping for both bed and breakfast.

Despite their itchy paws, neither Marmaduke nor Skimbleshanks have ever been known to enter the cathedral building. Recently, however, incriminating evidence has been produced which suggests otherwise. Two distinctive sets of muddy pawprints were to be seen, tracing circles on the altar vestments in the Lady Chapel. No doubt Marmaduke and Skimbleshanks would swear that they had been shopping at the time.

En route to the pet shop

LEFT: *Skimbleshanks on the trail of the rabbit*

Gorbachev & Whippy

Piebald Gorbachev and Whippy the tabby enjoy
a particular distinction as cathedral cats. As far as we
can ascertain, they alone have had an architectural
feature incorporated specifically for their use.

Gorbachev the glutton?

The cathedral architect had designed new walls and gates for the Chatfields' house, adjoining the main gates to the cathedral close. As this left no thoroughfare for the two cats, the architect designed a tiny gothic arch at pavement height. Visitors are sometimes startled as Gorbachev's head emerges, as if by magic, from the wall.

Gloucester Cathedral shows a great many signs of its Norman origins – particularly in the crypt – although the transepts, presbytery and South Aisle were substantially remodelled in the fourteenth century in striking early Perpendicular style. The fan vaulting dates back to this period too, and is the oldest standing example. The fifteenth century saw the building of the Lady Chapel, considered by many to be the finest of its kind.

Gorbachev joined the Chatfields when they were living in Hampshire. Daughter Elizabeth arrived home from a college friend's house one day with Gorbachev in her arms. The family had just acquired Whippy (thus named for his twitching tail), and the two cats together were almost compensation for the one they had just lost. Together they haunted the nearby tidal creek, until the Chatfields moved to Gloucester Cathedral.

Gorbachev showed greater territorial aspirations than his Soviet namesake. First he adopted the entire cathedral close, before extending his domain to take in the supermarket and the fish and chip shop. Soon all those who came to eat a picnic lunch in the peace of the cathedral precincts became aware that they had no alternative but to share their food with Gorbachev. He could charm it out of anybody. In the space of one day he was spotted sitting between two boys eating chips from both of them, and an hour later was helping two ladies to finish off their respective danish pastries.

One day Mrs Chatfield was most startled to see Gorbachev gulping down some sausages. He had managed to convince one old gentleman – who was

in the process of posting his letters in the cathedral post box – that he was starving. The old gentleman turned to Mrs Chatfield, remarking how shameful it was that people didn't feed their cats properly. Given that his sausages were by now no more than a memory, she restrained herself from telling him that Gorbachev had, not five minutes since, finished both his and Whippy's daily meal.

On the day of our appointment, Gorbachev spent quite a while trying to swat my camera off its tripod. Either he was sure that I had food inside it, or he was trying to tell me that he would only consent to be photographed in return for some suitable edible reward.

For cats with dramatically different characters, Gorbachev and Whippy have an unusual and close relationship. Although Whippy is shy, they spend a lot of time together, playing in the garden overlooking the West porch of the cathedral, sleeping in a tight bundle, or incessantly washing each other. When Gorbachev became ill with an unknown virus, he would sit, head drooping on the floor, by the kitchen stove. Whippy hardly ever left his side, sitting by him with both paws wrapped gently round his sick companion, moving only to allow Gorbachev to be fed by syringe.

Despite the vet's gloomy prognosis, Gorbachev survived, and is still managing to persuade local people out of their food.

LEFT: *The cathedral cat's thoroughfare*

RIGHT: *A demure Whippy*

Princess

Princess arrived at her new home a pauper.
Hungry and maltreated, she had been languishing
in the local animal sanctuary. Little could she have
known that soon she would be a cathedral
cat with an Eton education.

Princess was rescued at the age of eighteen months for Cathryn, daughter of Hereford's Head Verger, Michael Bayliss. She began by finishing off a large plate of liver, giving herself a good wash, and putting her bad experiences quickly behind her. At the time the Baylisses lived in Shropshire. Soon afterwards they moved to the peaceful Vicars Cloister at Hereford

The Princess and the pear tree

Cathedral and thence to Eton, one of Britain's most prestigious public schools in the county of Berkshire, where Michael was Verger to the chapel.

Princess is an outside cat, and so accompanied each of the journeys to her new abodes by caterwauling non-stop for up to three hours. Although she settled into each home very well, she was clearly more suited to the rural character of Shropshire and Herefordshire.

In the urban environment of Eton Princess came to grief when she was badly injured by construction traffic at a nearby building site. With careful treatment she, like Biggles at Westminster, made a miraculous recovery, in time to join the Bayliss family when they moved back to Hereford.

The cathedral, first built in 676 on the banks of the River Wye, is striking for the use of pink sandstone. As one of the cathedrals that hosts the annual Three Choirs Festival, it occupies a special place in the cultural life of Britain, further enhanced by the superb chained library and the world-famous 'Mappa Mundi', a thirteenth century map of the world, showing a flat earth with Jerusalem at its centre.

The Baylisses recall how, when they moved yet again, to a different house in the same cloisters, Princess sat nostalgically outside the door of their old house for days. She then discovered that the wall of their new garden adjoined the gardens of the Bishop's Palace. These gardens, which include a long stretch of the River Wye, make for the most superb hunting territory.

One of Princess's favourite spots is a branch in an old yew tree, which overhangs the river, and she will sit for hours, watching the river slip by beneath and doubtless spotting the occasional bank vole. I had to

explore the gardens thoroughly with one of the gardeners to try to locate Princess after she decided that she'd had enough of me when we were in the Vicars Cloister. She was nowhere to be found.

Her prowls in the Chapter Garden and the cloisters are slightly more traumatic. Winston, the cathedral organist's boisterous and very friendly puppy, is always more excited to see Princess than she is to see him and, as a result, Princess spends rather more time up the old pear tree than she would otherwise have chosen. To her chagrin, the branches have recently been lopped.

Since joining the Bayliss family, Princess has gradually learned to trust outsiders, and although she can still be wary, will now occasionally accept a stroke from a tourist. She will even wander over to the North entrance of the cathedral, waiting for her family to come out, so she can saunter at their heels back to the shelter of her tranquil cloister home.

ABOVE: *A rare still moment*

LEFT: *The quickest way back from Palace Gardens*

RIGHT: *The cloisters — but where is Winston?*

Marcus Aurelius

Toast the tom cat has been deported
from Lincoln Cathedral for spraying in the aisle.
Now that he is gone, Marcus is a very relaxed cat, able
without interruption to indulge his favourite pastime
of eating the strongest and most pungent blue
cheese he can get his paws on.

Marcus belongs to Mrs Maureen Bone, now school Matron at the Cathedral School, who cares for orphaned cats as well as she cares for the choristers. Some ten years ago, as matron to Oundle school, she saw an advertisement in her local paper for a half-Persian, quarter-Burmese kitten, which had been rejected by his mother. She already had two cats – Buttons and Lucy – but couldn't ignore a cat in need.

She remembers the first sight of Marcus, a tiny ball of brown fur, sitting dejectedly on the table in a tiny kitchen. With no hesitation, she scooped him up into the front of her anorak and walked home through the town.

To her relief, Buttons, Lucy and the rapidly growing Marcus got on famously. Eventually, however, Buttons died and Mrs Bone took up her present position in Lincoln. At first her cats were reluctant to go out. She trained them to walk on leads, which they seemed thoroughly to enjoy until, with inhibitions lost, they ventured out by themselves to explore their new cathedral environment.

The cathedral grounds at Lincoln are overlooked by the central tower, the highest in England. The only remaining Norman sections of the building, built by Remigius, the first post-Conquest bishop, are the richly ornamented lower parts of the West Front, and the bottom sections of the two West towers. St Hugh, bishop of Lincoln, started much of the replacement building work, in an early Gothic style contemporary with that of Hereford Cathedral. There are two awe-inspiring circular windows, 'The Dean's Eye' and 'The Bishop's Eye', in the thirteenth century transepts. The cathedral also has a particularly fine library designed by Christopher Wren.

Driven off by football

After Marcus's arrival Mrs Bone rescued another cat, Sally. Marcus, appearing to remember his own unhappy beginnings, and the kindness with which he was taken into Mrs Bone's family, tried to become a surrogate parent. He adopted Sally with ferocious affection, pinning her down with one paw firmly around her neck, whilst remorselessly washing and grooming her. Even

LEFT: *Visiting Lucy's burial place*

RIGHT: **The last sight of Marcus**

now, Marcus and Sally curl up to sleep wrapped around one another. Unlike Marcus, however, Sally remains a cautious cat, very wary of anyone but her owner.

Lucy, meanwhile, had adopted the cathedral school, accompanying the caretaker on his rounds, and sitting quietly in the headmaster's maths lessons. She made some good friends amongst the cathedral school staff — in particular the House Master, the Head of English, whom she regularly joins in the school staffroom.

Whilst Lucy paraded around the school, Marcus kept a low profile, staying for the most part in the Matron's apartments. However, when Lucy died, he came out, and took over almost all Lucy's territory

and habits, perhaps spurred on in the knowledge that the caretaker always finished his morning rounds with breakfast. His particular friend is Mrs Varney, the Latin teacher, which is not surprising for a cat named after a Roman emperor and philosopher.

Not as committed to academic pursuits, Marcus prefers to wait by the cloister door for the choristers to return from singing practice in the cathedral. In the middle of our photographic session, however, the choristers came out to play football. Marcus was perhaps reminded of a bad experience with a football, because he disappeared around the cathedral, not to be seen for the rest of the day.

Samuel

It is lucky that Samuel and another tabby –
Westminster's Biggles – have never met, because
one is from Lancashire, the other from Yorkshire.
Given that they are two of the toughest customers
in this book, a feline War of the Roses would
no doubt have ensued.

Samuel journeyed to Peterborough from the Lancashire village smallholding where he was born by train. He thoroughly enjoyed the experience, but then to see him curled up in front of the fire, it is hard to imagine anything bothering him very much.

In fact he views the cathedral as a kind of stone farm, full of opportunities for hunting. Visitors are sometimes startled to see this sleek tabby darting out from the portico pillars of the West doors, to leap on some hapless pigeon which had mistaken Samuel for a gargoyle.

His home is one of the most important Norman buildings in England, constructed using the local Barnack stone. Samuel's house looks over the West Front, an imposing and beautiful example of Early English Gothic construction. The painted ceiling of the cathedral is considered to be one of the most significant works of ecclesiastical art in existence. Katherine of Aragon, Henry VIII's first wife, is buried here and Peterborough was the original resting place of Mary Queen of Scots.

When Samuel's owner, Deputy Head Verger Keith Nelson, was Bishop's Verger, Samuel did nothing to help his career prospects. Rather he used to chase the Bishop's hens around the garden.

However, turkey is his favourite quarry – the oven-ready variety. At Christmas, Keith puts the turkey in the oven, and Samuel stands, back against the oven door until the turkey is removed. Naturally Samuel gets the first cut. It is doubtful if I could have got any pictures of Samuel at all if it hadn't been for Keith's kindness in accompanying me for hours with a large bag of turkey scraps.

Outside the Deanery door

RIGHT: *Pigeon watching at the West Front*

LEFT: *Samuel in the West Porch*

Sam has some pretty definite ideas about food on the whole. Just below turkey in his list of favourite snacks comes garlic and herb mayonnaise, followed closely by pastrami with black pepper. He also has a passion for raw eggs. Keith swears that he can crack an egg in the kitchen and the sound will bring Sam bursting wildly into the kitchen from anywhere, even outside.

Samuel rules the cathedral precincts with an easy authority. The other cats know him as serious trouble, and all keep well away. During the summer when the close is often packed with people eating picnic lunches, Samuel will stalk around the perimeter ignoring everyone, even those with turkey or pastrami sandwiches.

Yet it would be misleading to talk of Samuel as a cat who only walks on the wild side, for he is also devoted to his owner. He used to accompany him in the many formal cathedral processions. If Keith is in the cathedral, Samuel will sometimes sit and cry outside. If he is outside the door on duty, then Samuel will just sit beside him.

LEFT: Practising
the gargoyle pose

RIGHT: Moving
in on a pigeon

Samuel always meets his owner coming off cathedral duty, usually springing onto his shoulder for a ride back home. When they arrive he likes to have what Keith mildly refers to as a 'mad half hour', in which the floor rugs are dragged around the room and the furniture is rearranged. During this time Keith advises visitors to keep their ankles well clear of the floor.

Even at bedtime, Samuel rules the roost. At the end of an exhausting cathedral day, he will jump up next to Keith, and push and nudge him until Keith vacates what is clearly Samuel's rightful place on the settee.

Ambrose

Canon Colin Slee is often reminded of the
old adage 'more haste, less speed', when he grabs
at the cassock which rests on a chair in his hallway.
A startled Ambrose may fly through the air, or
hang on in sleepy bewilderment as he is
whirled out of the front door.

Ambrose: no sign of the pot belly

Ambrose, who can't think of a better place to snooze, has the 'heart of a farm cat', according to Canon Slee. He was found by the Slees on a farm, during a visit to the Cotswold village of Great Tew. Their old cat Enoch had recently died, and the jet black Ambrose was acquired as consolation for daughters Ruth and Rachael.

Ambrose's new home St Alban's was originally the largest of the English monastic churches, becoming a parish church after the dissolution of the monasteries and a cathedral in 1877. Inside the building is appealingly simple, retaining an impressive Norman severity. The central tower is the only one in England built of brick, including Roman bricks. In the nave are delightful mural paintings dating from the twelfth and thirteenth centuries and a beautiful graffito of a cat.

In spite of his provenance, Ambrose never had any trouble settling into cathedral life, although his eccentric habits were evident right from the start. He had an insatiable appetite for tea and biscuits and a pot belly to match. He was also fascinated by the bees that Canon Slee kept on the kitchen roof, and would sit for hours watching them fly in and out of their hive. Although he made no attempt to interfere, they eventually got fed up with this unwavering attention. Ambrose was seen leaping off the roof and into the nearest clump of bushes, surrounded by a determined and irritated posse of bees. He now steers well clear of any bee hive.

Ambrose quickly discovered that Sumpter Yard, which connects the old part of town to the cathedral building, was a marvellous place to wait for people

Casting a nether eye

Refreshment in the canonry garden

coming in and out of the cathedral, and it soon became his pastoral role to greet everyone with tail held high. For Ambrose, however, like other cats in this book, the cathedral doors present no obstacle. He is often seen strolling down the nave, or washing himself in the transept.

Although Ambrose enjoys the undivided affection of the Slees, he has a special friend. A litter of feral kittens were discovered in the grounds, most of which were distributed to various members of the congregation (having been given suitable names such as Episcopus, Magnificat, Catachumen and Catolick). Ambrose's friend was given away, and renamed Timmy. Perhaps Timmy preferred a more ecclesiastical name. He certainly decided he was happier at the cathedral, and to Ambrose's delight made his own way back. The two cats spend long happy hours in the grounds, mostly stalking and sometimes catching squirrels.

Generally a healthy cat, Ambrose tore a claw one day. When the vet had bandaged his leg, Ambrose was returned with strict instructions that he should stay indoors for several days. However, a day of Ambrose pleading to be let out drove the Slee family to desperate measures. Canon Slee hit on an unconventional but highly effective way of weatherproofing the damaged limb. Thus it was that Ambrose could be seen each day for a fortnight, limping round the cathedral yard with a condom covering his injured leg.

RIGHT: *Ambrose: 'the heart of a farm cat'*

Chan & SaliMali

You would expect a Siamese cat with such
exotic names as Tibaan Repens, Wyely Trendsetter and
Avena Tobias in his pedigree to cut quite a dash. So it is
with Chan. He is named after the Duke of Chandos but, if
the Lewises had accepted the advice of their Chinese
friends, it would have been far more complicated.

His home is at St Davids, the only non-English cathedral in this book, and the only one with an essentially rural setting, in a grassy hollow beneath the village-like city of St Davids, adjoining open fields. Built by Dewi Sant, a missionary monk who became Wales' patron saint, pilgrims have been coming here for a thousand years. In its heyday, two pilgrimages to St Davids were equivalent to one to Rome. The present building was constructed in the late twelfth century, and has been added to since.

Like all Siamese cats, Chan expected to be pampered from an early age. He quickly discovered that the drying rack above the cooker was particularly cosy and almost cooks himself to a turn when taking his daily nap. If it hadn't been for the arrival of Sali, he would probably have become intolerably stuck-up.

Sali has rather more obscure origins. Whilst walking back from the cathedral to the deanery one day, the Dean thought he heard mewing. It took him some while to spot three ginger and white kittens tucked in a hole in the garden wall. He brought them back to the house, where they were greeted with great joy by the children, Non, John and Christa. SaliMali is named after a little old lady in one of daughter Christa's old reading books, but is always known as plain Sali.

Given the age difference between the cats, and Chan's snootiness, it was a surprise to everyone when the two cats struck up such a boisterous friendship. They leapt through the house with gay abandon, swatting each other good naturedly.

Even when Sali made a beeline for Chan's dozing place above the cooker things didn't end in tears. Rather it began a battle of wits which continues to this day. The agile Sali usually manages to beat Chan

The dashing Chan

to the drying rack. Chan then sits nonchalantly on the side of the stove, pretending not to notice. When an opportunity presents itself, he jumps into the gap between Sali and the wall, easing Sali off with his superior weight.

My morning's conversation with the Lewises was punctuated by one or other cat leaping across the room to deliver a playful cuff to each other. SaliMali eventually tired of this and began to drag my tape recorder around by the strap, patting the moving tape spool. SaliMali also led the way outside for the photography, luring Chan from his perch up on the cooker.

Although Sali occasionally wanders around the ruins of the Bishop's Palace, and Chan has once or twice been spotted, yowling loudly, near the cathedral, they mainly stay in the walled gardens of the deanery. Sali

LEFT: *A fragrant interlude for SaliMali*

RIGHT: *Back into the fray*

leaps energetically up and down every available tree while Chan ambles leisurely through the grass.

Water fascinates Sali, and as a kitten she would spend long periods standing with her front paws immersed in a bowl of water. When they visit the deanery, grandchildren Emily and Cerys aren't so reluctant to have their baths when they know that the cat will be prowling up and down the edge.

She is also a hunter of some distinction, bringing in a succession of live mice and sometimes a mole. Mrs Lewis sweeps the unfortunate rodents into a dustpan and deposits them, somewhat bemused but none the worse for wear, back out in the garden.

Chan's predilection is for travel. If he can get into any car parked at the deanery, he will stretch out on the parcel shelf and go to sleep. On at least three occasions an uncontrite Chan has been returned to the deanery after an unplanned trip through the village. One unwitting driver only became aware of Chan's presence on one of these jaunts after a good few miles when he noticed the tail in his rear view mirror, swishing to and fro like a wiper.

Dennis

Dennis is a regular visitor to the cathedral
stonemason's yard, from which he returns, covered
in stone dust, looking for all the world like the
feline spectre of St Paul's.

He arrived as a kitten at St Paul's Cathedral three years ago, one chilly Christmas. Some students staying in the Dean's house presented him as a gift to fill the gap left by the loss of Wooters, the family's previous cat, who had come up with them from Gloucestershire.

Little did Dennis know that his territory would be the precincts of one of Britain's finest buildings. Reconstructed over a period of some thirty-four years by Christopher Wren, after the old cathedral was destroyed in the Fire of London, St Paul's is considered by many to be his finest achievement. It does of course have an extensive history of royal and military pomp and ceremony.

Dennis rapidly formed a close friendship with Ruffin, the youngest of three prize winning border collies, and was soon exploring his new home with gusto. He is a companionable cat, insisting on being let in to any social gathering in the house. During the day he is equally at home lolling in the middle of the Dean's desk, or in the office, where he will sit watching Joan, the Dean's secretary. He finds great fascination in the clattering of the daisy wheel on her printer, and has been known to set it off himself while her back is turned.

Dennis was one of the first cathedral cats to discover that mice had nested in my old camera bag, and decided that he could be extremely comfortable snuggled down at the bottom, amongst film cartons and other bits and pieces. When he emerged he was affable to the extent of hopping on to my knee in the car, apparently keen to travel to my next destination – Ely.

The jaunty Dennis has one great problem. He cannot miaow. At best he produces a pitiful squeak. This can

The affable Dennis and sundial

be a great problem for him, for of all the cats in this book, he is the most intrepid explorer – a Ranulph Fiennes of the cat world. He once spent two days in the spare bathroom airing cupboard, and is always getting shut in Joan's stationery cupboard.

His pioneering spirit takes him far beyond his home turf. He strolls much of the City of London at night, heading down towards the river, and visiting many famous City sites. His worst moment was to be trapped in a nearby empty building for six days. He must have heard the voices and sounds of his family passing each night, walking the dogs. As luck would have it, some utility workers spotted him and the Dean recalls how, when he went to bring him back, Dennis sprang into his arms, wrapping his front paws tightly round his neck as they walked back to the safety of Amen Court.

Earlier in his life Dennis went missing for two days and was found by the Dean late one night, stuck up a tree in the cathedral churchyard. The Dean didn't feel equal to the climb himself and, noticing a light on in the music master's room at the school, he rang the bell. When the music master opened the door, the Dean apologized for interrupting him so late at night, and then enlisted him to shin up the tree to rescue Dennis. The music master did at least have the presence of mind to enquire of the Dean, as he clambered up the tree, whether they might discuss new salary scales.

The Dean's study: Dennis and Ruffin the collie

RIGHT: Dennis at home in Amen Court

Simpkin

Simpkin was originally called
'Vacance de Vélo'. This odd name commemorated
a family cycling holiday in France.

Simpkin in the cloisters

When her owners, the family of the curate of All Hallows, Wellingborough, Northamptonshire, were appointed to a position overseas, 'Vacance' moved to live with Stephen Abbott, a lay vicar of Salisbury Cathedral, his wife Kate and their two children Rachel and Richard.

The cathedral is set in a magnificent site, surrounded by lawns, with water meadows leading down to the river, and close fringed with buildings of different periods. Trollope is believed to have conceived the idea for his first Barchester novel here. The building followed a complete Gothic plan and accordingly has a remarkable sense of architectural unity. Although the stonework is austere, with purbeck marble columns and cream coloured Chilmark stone, the building has an inspiring internal height of eighty feet and, of course, Britain's highest spire, a spectacular edifice newly restored after the cathedral's well-publicized appeal.

As soon as 'Vacance' arrived in Salisbury, she was renamed Simpkin, after the cat in Beatrix Potter's *The Tailor of Gloucester*, and joined one of her two kittens,

A pause on the daisy-strewn grass

Portia, who had been born in a hat under a bed at Wellingborough. Once reunited, mother and daughter cat took absolutely no notice of one another.

The family eventually moved to the cathedral precincts, from their house on the other side of Salisbury. The first thing Simpkin did was to wander back from the Cathedral Close to her old home, walking brazenly across busy roads showing a total disdain for the traffic.

After the move, she seemed determined never to let the family out of her sight, for fear that they might move again. She walks with Kate Abbott and the two children on their way to school. She doesn't go into the school, but simply waits by the road crossing for the whole day. If the family goes home by a different route, Kate frequently has to go back to the road crossing to collect Simpkin too. However, as Simpkin runs alongside her bicycle, this can be done fairly quickly. If she does decide not to go out with the family, she'll sometimes wait with the Cathedral Close constables until they return.

When the Abbotts and I wandered around after Simpkin, she promenaded around at a steady pace with barely a pause. As soon as I saw an interesting background or setting, she had walked past.

On the rare day that she trusts the family to return, Simpkin will go to hunt rabbits in the water meadows or visit the works staff in the stone yard. Like other cats in this book, she has the run of the precinct and the cathedral itself. She stops to be photographed and petted by visitors and, if she feels that not enough

ABOVE: *By the perimeter wall*
RIGHT: *Heading for the organist's windowsill*

attention has been given her, she waits at the West End door until someone stops to admire her.

Occasionally she joins the family at the morning service. Her most celebrated appearance was on Palm Sunday. Simpkin decided that if the cathedral could have a donkey in the procession, they could most certainly have a cat, and stuck determinedly by the donkey's heels from start to finish.

She is not, however, as pious as she looks. When the children go to Sunday school, Simpkin goes along too – not, it has to be said, for her own edification, but rather to taunt Taffy, the organist's dog. He has to watch through the window in excruciating frustration, whilst Simpkin hops on and off the windowsill, testing exactly how angry a dog can get when teased by a cathedral cat.

Bill & Benjamina

An evening visitor to the Coles house in Truro
will either find four animals – two cats and two dogs –
snuggled up in a heap on the sofa, or the cats Bill and
Benjamina asleep on the lap of a jolly-looking
rabbit made by Mrs Cole.

When Head Verger Mr Cole and his wife Maureen went to look for two new cats they were spoilt for choice. The farmyard they visited was teeming with about fifty felines, not to mention nine dalmatians.

Eventually they chose two, but catching them was another matter. Every time the Coles pounced, the cats were one step ahead. After two hours trying, the farmer's wife took pity and offered to deliver the cats later in the week to the cathedral.

The Coles live right under the shadow of the cathedral building, whose three spires tower imposingly over the nearby narrow streets. The building is late Victorian but appears much older on first sight. It is a symbol for many local people of the county of Cornwall's claims to independence since before its construction there had been a combined diocese of Devon and Cornwall.

When Bill and Benjamina arrived, Bill immediately resumed his old tricks. He shot to the top of the curtains where he remained for two hours, swishing his tail and glaring down. Although he progressed from the curtains to the top of the water heater, and spent

Bill descends from the garden wall

LEFT: *Benjamina —
shy and home-loving*

RIGHT: *Benjamina's
eyrie on the stairs*

a considerable amount of time there, he is now a floppy and highly affectionate cat who is happy to spend hours having his chin tickled.

Like some other cats in this book, he is a television watcher, with a preference for snooker matches and wildlife. When he ventures out of the house, it is to dig up as many plants as he can find in the cathedral precincts. His muddy nose gives him away every time.

Benjamina came more quietly, as befits a long haired tabby female. She rarely leaves the house, preferring to gaze intently out of the window for hours from the half landing on the stairs. She is of a more nervous disposition than Bill and will shoot for cover at the merest whiff of a stranger.

Benjamina actually crept out of cover while I was talking to the Coles and allowed me to tickle her stomach. For some reason she didn't find me threatening, and even permitted herself to be carried up to her normal lookout post on the landing to be pho-

tographed. Bill came outside, but it was a busy time in the precincts and no sooner had he clambered up onto the wall than he would dash along it, alarmed at the sight and sound of so many people.

Mr and Mrs Coles arrived in Cornwall with two ginger and white tom cats called Sammy and Joey. They were veterans of cathedral life, having lived at St Mary's, in Bristol for many years. Although the balmy climate of Cornwall seemed to suit them, the Coles remember a call one night from a stranger in the neighbouring town of St Austell, some fifteen miles away, asking them whether they had lost a cat called Sammy. The caller explained that he had arrived home after a visit to Truro, and was just about to lock his car when he noticed a large white cat curled up asleep on the back seat. Maybe Sammy had been trying to get back to Bristol. There were no long term ill effects: Sammy and Joey thrived at Truro until they died at the good old age of nineteen.

Cordelia & Fanny

Cordelia recently disappeared for a week,
much to the distress of her owner Chris Reynolds.
It transpired that she had been at the local
Conservative Club, nailing her political colours
firmly to the mast.

Cordelia on Treacle's territory

Fanny's epic journey continues into the Close

Chris had spent his university years in a house with the more prosaically named Baggage. When he was appointed as maths teacher at Wells Cathedral School he made an early visit to the Cat Protection League in Taunton. He came away with a small coal-black kitten.

The cathedral precincts make wonderful cat territory. They are calm and secluded, and the building itself doesn't dominate the town in the manner of some cathedrals. The West Front, embellished with statues of over four hundred saints, prophets and angels, overlooks a spacious and tranquil green. The famous 'scissor arches' dominate the nave.

Vicars Close, where Chris and Cordelia live, is one of the best preserved medieval streets in Europe. First the two shared a small apartment, and then moved to a

larger house from which Cordelia steadfastly refused to go out, despite being posted daily through the cat flap. Chris diagnosed loneliness on the part of his cat and decided to find her a companion.

The new cat, named Francesca, is also jet black but marginally smaller than Cordelia. She is a fourth generation cat from the Close, whose mother, grandmother and great-grandmother were called respectively, Custard,

'Fanny never goes anywhere'

Treacle and Pippin. Francesca was deemed by Chris to be too dignified a name for such a naughty cat, and he shortened it to Fanny. Both cats are named after well-known cooks.

The two cats got on well together until Fanny was speyed. Nowadays, for no apparent reason, Cordelia growls at Fanny whenever she comes near, and Fanny jumps on Cordelia's back when she's asleep. Fanny is the scourge of Chris's office. If she wants attention when he is marking, she swats papers off the desk and grabs at the end of his pen.

The two cats have the cobbled Vicars Close to themselves, but there are at least fourteen other related cats all staking territorial claims. The only cat which makes incursions into other territories is Tablet, a litter mate of Fanny's, who went so far as to come through the cat flap into the house, sending both Cordelia and Fanny bounding up the stairs in terror.

Perhaps for this reason Fanny doesn't usually go further than a small bump in the front lawn, know as 'The little Hill of Herman'. In contrast Cordelia avails herself of the entire cathedral precinct. Having been assured by Chris that Fanny would simply sit decoratively on the 'Little Hill of Herman', I was perturbed to see her disappear down the Close, through the archway and out of sight for the first time ever. In contrast Cordelia, whom I wanted to photograph in front of the West Front, steadfastly refused to leave the Close.

A wary Cordelia in Vicars Close

Cordelia regularly attends choir practice, and sits in fascination, watching the choristers and voluntary choir practising in the undercroft. She attends services too, particularly evensong, and is regularly brought back to the house by the Head Verger, who lives next door.

She rather startled the Bishop one day when, at the end of a funeral service, whilst giving the final blessing, he glanced down to find her demurely tucked at his feet, gazing sympathetically at the mourners.

Biggles

Biggles – a cathedral cat for five years up until
the autumn of 1992 – now lives in Tamworth. He was
removed from the cathedral precincts on the orders of the
Receiver General after letting one too many tourists know
that he didn't welcome their attentions.

A notice went up in the solarium passage seeking a new home for him, with another next to it campaigning for remission of his sentence. But one sad day he was taken away, never to stalk the Abbey cloisters again.

Biggles began life as a farm cat. He came from the neighbouring village to Frickley in Yorkshire where the cats, like the colliers, come tough. Dick Webb, himself a miner, wife Sheila and daughter Toby took him as a hand-sized kitten when their previous cat vanished.

In 1988 Dick and Sheila took up the post of Custodian Caterers at Westminster Abbey. The Abbey is of course the coronation church of the sovereigns of England, the final resting-place of many, the tomb-house of national heroes and heroines as well as a triumph of singularly

Tigger of the Yard

beautiful Gothic architecture. Not actually a cathedral, because it doesn't have a bishop, the first major Abbey building was begun by Edward the Confessor in 1050 and finished shortly before his death in 1065. The funeral at the Abbey Church is depicted in the Bayeux tapestry. The current building was constructed between 1245 and 1269 under Henry II, who was buried inside. Various additions were made in the succeeding centuries, including the beautiful Perpendicular Henry VII Chapel at the East End, and the twin towers of the West Front, built by Wren and finished by his illustrious pupil, Hawksmoor.

It took a while until Biggles 'found his feet', in Dick's words, at Westminster Abbey. A marauding black and white cat dealt out a series of severe beatings to him.

Hunter and pugilist

An early morning Biggles...

...begins his rounds

Once this cat was vanquished, Biggles reigned supreme. With paws like boxing gloves and more cuts than Coriolanus, he terrorized rats, cats, dogs and humans in equal measure.

His chief protagonist was Benjie, the King Charles spaniel belonging to the Neary family. Living up to his name as a flying hero, Biggles would launch himself from the Virginia creeper outside the cloisters onto the back of the unfortunate dog. The other cats – among them the Fergusons' Thumbs and the Sempers' Spike and Jelly – became increasingly neurotic. The wives of the clergy, armed with brooms and water shooters, tried to fight him off in vain.

Dick Webb puts Biggles' nasty streak down to being shot with an airgun as a kitten. Apparently he would roll over and allow his tummy to be tickled before. Then in 1991 he was crushed by a car outside the Houses of Parliament. He was given a one in ten thousand chance of walking again, but came back, and meaner with it. When the vet operated on him he found one of the airgun pellets lodged under his spine. The Abbey duly commemorated his return by carving a new gargoyle in the image of Biggles on the restored tower.

In the same year Biggles ripped first the trousers of an overfriendly male police constable, and then the tights

RIGHT: *Biggles on guard*

An unfortunate invitation to the unwary tourist

of a woman police constable. On that occasion he received an official warning. Biggles simply didn't like to be molested. For some reason the Americans and the French suffered worse. The Japanese seemed, however, to guess that his vanity was as strong as his irritability. He would parade before their video cameras with his tail held characteristically high.

His daily 'circuit' of the Abbey precincts was well-known. It would usually take him right through the Abbey itself. On Tuesday there would be breakfast at College Hall and, most days, lunch at Up School. One day he entered the Abbey during evensong as the choir was in full flight. He stood beside the Director of Music and joined in. The voices of the boys in the choir quickly began to quaver with laughter.

Often to be found sleeping under the altar, or sharpening his claws on its side, Biggles was one day used by Canon Semper as illustration for his sermon at the children's Christmas crib service. He asked Dick to try to get Biggles to join the crib scene. Instead Biggles walked determinedly out down the main aisle. There were many occasions too when the Beadle would open the Abbey in the morning only for a sleepy Biggles to emerge, having somehow avoided setting off the ultra-sensitive alarms.

Although Dick, Sheila and Toby miss Biggles and can't bring themselves to visit him, they know that he has settled quickly into his Tamworth home. His new guardians had never allowed a cat indoors until Biggles protested loudly and eventually took over a whole bedroom for himself. He overcame his fear of the farm geese, and within days had joined forces with them.

Recently the family moved off the farm and into a house with an acre and a half of garden. Very quickly they heard from their neighbour. 'Do you own a large tabby cat?' he said. 'It's just sorted out my dog.'

Sheba & Min

Sheba arrived at her family's new house in
Winchester feeling a bit put out, as she had climbed
into a packing case at her old house and been loaded
into the removal truck along with the furniture.

Sheba and Min on the old cloister wall

Sheba and Min are mother and daughter, and are twelve and ten years old respectively. They live with the Archdeacon of Basingstoke Alec Knight and his wife Sheelagh in a large Queen Anne house within the precincts of Winchester Cathedral.

The Cathedral is rich in history, the longest medieval building 'north of the Alps'. The Saxon kings of Wessex worshipped here, and it has been a bishop's see since 679. The present cathedral is still substantially Norman Romanesque, although the present tower was built in the twelfth century after the original collapsed. The nave interior was recast with the original Norman pillars being encased in stonework of the Perpendicular style.

Sheba came to the Knights when they lived in Warwickshire and she was already pregnant. She had been confined to a garage after her original owner developed an allergy to cats. The family kept two of the litter, Mops and Min – short for Mini-cat as she bore more than a passing resemblance to her mother.

There were originally three cats and one dog – Gemma – who all grew up in the Hampshire village to which the Knights moved. Min's brother Mops disappeared one day, in the way of many cats, and was never seen again. When Gem died both cats grieved deeply, spending a great deal of time looking for her. There is a new dog now – Meg – whom both cats have known since she was a puppy.

Sheba is a cat who likes people, and will happily travel around lying firmly across one's shoulders, whilst Min is more obviously independent. One day Sheba disappeared without trace only for the family

Three animals which respond to a whistle

to find, after an extensive search, that she had been adopted by another family living near the cathedral. Sheelagh Knight remembers how happy Sheba was in her new temporary home, and how heartbroken the family's little boy was when Sheba returned to the Knights. The episode had a happy ending, however, for soon after Sheba's restoration to the canonry, a new kitten arrived for Sheba's young friend.

Min, who had thoroughly enjoyed the extra attention lavished on her during Sheba's absence, was not so pleased to see her mother return, and spent several days in a great sulk.

With an enormous walled garden, the two cats do not generally venture far within the cathedral precincts, but they do like to spend some time on the green in front of the house, peering down from the remains of the Norman cloister wall at passers-by. Perhaps because they have grown up with dogs, both Sheba and Min have a useful habit of responding to a whistle.

Sheba lay across my shoulders as I was interviewing Mrs Knight and, on replaying our taped conversations, I found that her purring almost drowned us out. As I tried to photograph Min in the walled garden behind the canonry, she sat on my camera bag and wouldn't be moved.

RIGHT: *The comfort of a cathedral home - Sheba and Min*

Tiger Lily Puccinella

Tiger Lily Puccinella is the Dean's cat
at Worcester, a position with a certain cachet and
status. Furthermore, she is the daughter of another
cathedral cat, Suleika of Westminster Abbey.

Tiger Lily's favourite wall

Suleika and her daughter Pushpah are legendary in the Church of England. They are a pure white pair which belong to the family of the late Canon Charles. Many a guest at their Abbey house was terrified as the two cats peered like small ghosts through the windows on winter nights. Amid gardens at the Abbey which were strangely infertile, the cats were the opposite, producing litter after litter of many-coloured kittens, all now highly prestigious pets. The former Dean, Edward Carpenter, has a ginger tom, Caspar. Giles Dawson, a master at the choir school has the diminutive Posnet. A jazz musician at Philip Larkin's funeral returned for a kitten which he named...Larkin.

Amongst all the many tens of kittens born to her cats, Mrs Charles remembers Tiger Lily as the most beautiful of a beautiful bunch, with a definite strain of Persian.

Dean Jeffery collected her on a visit to Church House, the administrative centre of the Church of England, which is situated alongside the Abbey. He remembers to this day the plaintive mewing that emanated from the catbox in the luggage rack on the train home.

Tiger Lily's home cathedral has a magnificent setting at the top of gardens which sweep down to the River Severn. Although the building dates from 1084, the great tower which is visible from miles around was not added until the fourteenth century. Home to the Three Choirs Festival, along with Hereford and Gloucester, the cathedral sees regular performances of the works of Edward Elgar, who lived in nearby Malvern and whose father, William Henry Elgar, had a local music shop and piano tuning business.

Although the Dean's children unceremoniously renamed their cat 'Kitty', Tiger Lily remains conscious of her position. Now seven years old, she disdains the cathedral itself, preferring to find prime positions on walls around the deanery where she can be easily admired. The only cloud in her sky is the presence of Sammy, burly with ginger and white stripes, who belonged to a previous housekeeper and who at the age of eleven is a kind of feline 'sitting tenant' in the deanery. Relations between the two cats are strained, but they consciously patrol different parts of the territory, so their paths rarely cross.

Tiger Lily was one of the cats who revelled in being 'posed' to have her picture taken. In fact she seemed to take quite a shine to me and, whilst Mrs Jeffrey and I were talking in the study, lay stretched out on my chest, chewing a large mouthful of my sweater.

She shows a winsome loyalty to her master, however, spending long periods sitting on his office desk. Occasionally she will paw pieces of paper onto the floor, although the Dean has yet to determine whether any specific criticism is implied. As other cats with pianos, Tiger Lily will sometimes tiptoe carefully across the keyboard of the Dean's word processor, leaving a trail of cat cypher across the screen. The Dean may only discover this when he is preaching a carefully prepared sermon. Maybe it is because his favourite cat fears his wrath that she never sleeps in the same place two nights running.

Atop the Dean's desk
RIGHT: *Tiger Lily: star of the catwalk*

Hippolytus

The Chancellor of York's cat once wrote a
complaining letter to the *Church Times*, asking
how some of his feline neighbours could be named
Hippolytus and Salome, whilst he was content
to be called Smudge. Presumably Smudge was even
more outraged to discover that Canon Mayland's
goat was called Hosannah.

Then again, York Minster is the largest medieval church in Northern Europe, and its animals have perhaps earned the right to go by names which match the dignity and grandeur of their home. Dating from 627, the first church on the site is believed to have been founded by Edwin, King of Northumbria; parts of the original structure still survive in the present building, which was constructed between 1220 and 1472. The visitor is struck by the wealth of stained glass and by the remarkable restoration undertaken after the recent fire.

Hippolytus, denizen of York, might be a social climber but he is also a pretty eccentric cathedral cat. It is rumoured that he was born in 1976, and whilst he may be old, he is still, as his owners Philip and Cathy Titcombe point out, going strong. He moved at ten weeks old from Appleton where the poet Andrew Marvell once lived to York, and shared a house by the river with a cat called Aristotle, with whom he became good friends. If Aristotle taught him to open the fridge door, he has a lot to answer for.

Hippo, as he is generally called, is an expert in the stealing of food, a cat burglar par excellence. When he and Philip moved to Worcester, Hippo was embroiled in what came to be known as the 'sausage affair', in which he ate one and a half pounds of sausages, including the wrapper.

This was followed by the 'pheasant episode', in which Hippolytus, desperately trying to gulp down a pheasant that he had borrowed, was pursued round the house with a broom.

Finally, there was the 'pigeon mishap', which came to light when Cathy noticed an odd smell pervading the

Hippo and the West Tower

house. A first search yielded nothing. Further and more urgent searches disclosed a late pigeon under Philip and Cathy's bed. When confronted with his misdemeanour, Hippo merely gave the cat equivalent of a bored shrug, and sauntered out into the cathedral close.

Hippo would begin a typical Worcester day with breakfast at home, before nipping over the wall to eat a further breakfast – that of the Dean's cat, Sammy. Then, fully replete, he would hop onto the Dean's desk and review the texts of any sermons that lay there.

When Philip became a songman at York, and the family moved into Precentors Court, the Minster began a decade of exposure to Hippo's ear-splitting night-time howling. The unearthly noise was even harnessed by Victor Lewis-Smith as a sound effect for his outrageous weekly local radio show and Hippolytus was duly featured in the *Radio Times*. So pained did he sound that several listeners sent in gifts of money for his welfare.

The Titcombes claim that Hippo, reared in a musical home, has an acute ear of his own. His preference, they say, is for early music, to the extent that he has

Daytime singing practice

RIGHT: *Lulled by Schubert*

been known to walk back from the Minster in disgust
if anything too modern was being sung or performed.
He is a regular fixture at the family's Saturday night
opera suppers.

A greeting from Hippolytus has been described
euphemistically by his owners as 'a friendly nip'. The
list of those who have received this dubious honour
continues to increase, and includes a Baronet's wife, a
photographer, the Emeritus Professor of Music at York
University, the piano tuner and various family friends.
He is still trying to add the Headmaster of the Minster
School to the list and obviously regarded me as fair
game too. He was pretty irritated about being taken
out onto the cathedral green, and when Cathy, Hippo
and I managed to meet up at the front door, he was
hatching revenge. For, when we settled into taking
photographs in the sitting room, he walked past me,
swatted my hand and nipped my wrist. I had been
warned.

In the autumn of his life, Hippolytus shows no
signs of retiring from his active life. There is still a
ladder in the hallway for the use of cat sitters, who
have regularly to retrieve him from the wall opposite,
where he sits happily howling the night away.

Hippo shows his
disdain for modern
music

The author and publishers would like
to thank the following for their help and cooperation
in making this book possible:-

Rex Hipple, BRISTOL CATHEDRAL

Dean and Mrs Simpson, CANTERBURY CATHEDRAL

Canon Jenkins, CARLISLE CATHEDRAL

Margaret Drury, CHRIST CHURCH, OXFORD

Mrs Mary Ford, COVENTRY CATHEDRAL

Sally, Sara and Paul Trepte, ELY CATHEDRAL

Canon and Mrs Chatfield, GLOUCESTER CATHEDRAL

Mr and Mrs Bayliss, HEREFORD CATHEDRAL

Mrs Bone, LINCOLN CATHEDRAL SCHOOL

Keith Nelson, PETERBOROUGH CATHEDRAL

Canon Colin Slee, ST ALBANS ABBEY

Dean and Mrs Lewis, ST DAVIDS CATHEDRAL

Dean and Mrs Evans, ST PAUL'S CATHEDRAL

Kate, Steven, Rachel and Richard Abbott, SALISBURY CATHEDRAL

Mr and Mrs Cole, TRURO CATHEDRAL

Chris Reynolds, WELLS CATHEDRAL

Dick and Sheila Webb, WESTMINSTER ABBEY

Canon and Mrs Knight, WINCHESTER CATHEDRAL

Dean and Mrs Jeffrey, WORCESTER CATHEDRAL

Philip and Cathy Titcombe, YORK MINSTER

Cathedral
cats

This charming book is a record of some of the most privileged cats in Britain – the cathedral cats.

Their homes could not be more ancient or more beautiful. They are admired by many thousands of tourists. There is hardly a door or a window which is closed to them. They have the run of the roofs and the vaults, the cloisters and the choir school, the nooks and the crannies.

Photographer Richard Surman travelled to twenty of the great cathedrals to record these fortunate felines. Here, in this unique and captivating book, is his photographic record of the cathedral cats.

UK £7.99*
CAN $17.00

ISBN 0-00-628071-4

00799>

*recommended price

9 780006 280712